# LOVE THYSELF

## THE MESSAGE FROM WATER III

# MASARU EMOTO

**HAY HOUSE, INC.**
Carlsbad, California
London • Sydney • Johannesburg
Vancouver • Hong Kong

**Published and distributed in the United States by:** Hay House, Inc., P.O. Box 5100, Carlsbad, CA 92018-5100 • *Phone:* (760) 431-7695 or (800) 654-5126 • *Fax:* (760) 431-6948 or (800) 650-5115 • www.hayhouse.com • **Published and distributed in Australia by:** Hay House Australia Pty. Ltd., 18/36 Ralph St., Alexandria NSW 2015 • *Phone:* 612-9669-4299 • *Fax:* 612-9669-4144 • www.hayhouse.com.au • **Published and distributed in the United Kingdom by:** Hay House UK, Ltd. • Unit 62, Canalot Studios • 222 Kensal Rd., London W10 5BN • *Phone:* 44-20-8962-1230 • *Fax:* 44-20-8962-1239 • www.hayhouse.co.uk • **Published and distributed in the Republic of South Africa by:** Hay House SA (Pty), Ltd., P.O. Box 990, Witkoppen 2068 • *Phone/Fax:* 27-11-706-6612 • orders@psdprom.co.za • **Distributed in Canada by:** Raincoast • 9050 Shaughnessy St., Vancouver, B.C. V6P 6E5 • *Phone:* (604) 323-7100 • *Fax:* (604) 323-2600

*Editorial supervision:* Jill Kramer  •  *Design:* Amy Gingery

*Translation:* Masayo Hachii
*Photography from IHM Research Institute:* Takashige Kizu, Seiko Ikeda, Hiroshi Oida, Takayuki Oshide, Takeshi Katsumata, Jun Futamura, Kouji Sakamoto, Masaya Sato, Migiwa Tanaka / *Photographs from Amana Images:* © Tsutomu Takasaki; © kanehisa Murakami; © Cross wave; © MasatoTokiwa; © Fumio Okita
Originally published by HADO Kyoikusha, Tokyo, Japan, in February of 2004

**Library of Congress Cataloging-in-Publication Data**

Emoto, Masaru, 1943-
 [Mizu karano dengon 3. English]
 Love thyself : the message from water III / Masaru Emoto.
   p. cm.
 ISBN-13: 978-1-4019-0899-7 (tradepaper)
 ISBN-10: 1-4019-0899-3 (tradepaper)
 1.  Water--Philosophy. 2.  Water--Religious aspects. 3.  Prayer.  I. Title: Message from water 3. II. Title: Love thyself. III. Title.
 RA591.5.E45613 2006
 363.6'1--dc22

2005017973

**ISBN 13:** 978-1-4019-0899-7
**ISBN 10:** 1-4019-0899-3

09  08  07  06   4  3  2  1
1st U.S. printing, January 2006

Printed in Singapore by Imago

# CONTENTS

Cont'd. on p. vi

# CONTENTS cont'd.

# PREFACE

## My Message from Water

It's been ten years since I developed the technique of frozen-water crystal photography. What began with one large refrigerator and one researcher has now become three refrigerators and six researchers, and the number of specimens has been increasing dramatically. More than anything, we're now able to obtain very stable results through our photographic techniques, and I believe that the quality of our work has shown great improvement.

After the publication of *The Message from Water* in June 1999, its popularity spread all over the world. It has been published in 23 languages as of January 2005, and thus has been able to attract keen interest from people around the globe. I now find myself receiving invitations to lecture worldwide—as of this printing I've been to 150 cities in 30 countries.

How did this happen? At the beginning I was so overwhelmed that I wasn't able to consider the reasons. But later, having met and talked to so many people from various places and after reading so many e-mails and letters, I now know the answer. And the more I understand, the more I realize the importance of my role. I often quiver with responsibility and burn with a sense of mission.

Here are some of the most fundamental reasons for the popularity of this work, although this list is by no means exhaustive. I've compiled the following from all the feedback I've received from the people who have attended my lectures or corresponded with me:

- The common language that the people of the world have been seeking is found in water crystals.

- Water has the ability to speak what's on our mind for us and awaken our subconscious memory.

- We can discern the origin, meaning, and importance of language through water crystals.

- These experiments help us understand why music heals people; and show us that paintings, sculptures, and other works of art truly have deeper meanings.

- This work helps us understand why alternative therapies exist and why they're effective.

- What we see in the crystal formations reinforces the fact that water is indispensable to the phenomenon of life.

- *The Message from Water* helps us understand religion and prayer, and it gives us a deeper sense of the relationship between humanity and the cosmos.

- Water crystals provide a clue to comprehending the nature of energy and what dimensionality is.

- Thanks to this work, we're one step closer to understanding the eternal theme of humanity that asks where we come from, why we're here, and what happens when we die.

In addition, I've heard comments from people that *The Message from Water* truly applies to everyday situations. These folks come from all walks of life and represent just about every industry: training organizations, agriculture, medicine, environmental consultation, food industries, clothing manufacturing, and so on.

About two years ago, my first grandchild was born. Naturally, he's an endearing and lovable child. (Pardon me for using my private pictures of him throughout the book!) One day I thought, *What state will the world be in when the children my grandson's age become adults?* I realized that we just can't leave things the way they are now. Thus, for the release of this third volume in my series *The Message from Water,* I decided to choose as a theme what the world most urgently needs at present: prayer. This is, of course, what's needed to eliminate war and terrorism throughout the world.

When I thought about it more deeply, I realized that prayer is most effectively sent when each person raises their energy of love by imagining a scene in which the people of the world are living in peace. I've learned this through the process of asking water many questions.

For this reason, I've selected *Love Thyself* as the title for this book. First, you must shine with positive, high-spirited vibrations, full of love. In order to do that, I think it's essential to love yourself, to be able to thank yourself, and to respect yourself. When you do so, each of these vibrations will be sent out into the cosmos, and the great symphony of that harmonic vibration will enfold our planet with waves, such as those that cherish your heaven-granted life.

This is my message from myself as water.

— **Masaru Emoto**

✳✳✳  ✳✳✳

# INTRODUCTION

## How It All Works

This book is essentially a photo album. I limited the amount of commentary on the crystal photos in the upcoming chapters since I thought it best to allow each reader to wonder and think for themselves. As the author and developer of the technique of crystal photography, however, there are actually many things I'd like to tell you about it. Indeed, the purpose of this book is to ask questions of water under the theme of prayer, and to convey to you my interpretations of the answers I obtained.

I prepared this introduction, therefore, to provide more detailed information on how the process works. I'd also like to visit the issue of the importance of prayer, its style, and the significance of words. And at the end of this section, for those who have accepted my ideas, I propose that we perform a prayer for world peace together. My prayer is what the title of this book eventually became: "Love Thyself."

For starters, I need to explain how this unique way of freezing water and taking pictures of crystals began.

### DISCOVERING THE MAGNETIC RESONANCE ANALYZER (MRA)

In November 1986, I had the chance to obtain the sales rights to the latest model of low-frequency medical therapy equipment developed in the United States. I became an independent general sales agent and established IHM (International Health Medical). I was 43 years old at the time.

The products were made in the USA, so I often visited California. My stateside counterpart was then Dr. Lee H. Lorenzen, who later developed microcluster water. He'd been searching for various cures for his wife, who was in poor health, and water ended up being his destination.

I resonated well with Dr. Lorenzen's personality and became attracted to his work with water. Having no background in science to begin with, all I could do was support his research. But the more I learned about water, the more clearly I realized that nothing had been revealed about the actual nature of this important substance. Wondering why, I investigated further and noticed that there was analyzing equipment to measure the *contents* of water, but none to measure water *quality*. Right away I talked to Dr. Lorenzen and asked him if we could find such equipment.

What I received was a piece of small machinery called a Bio Cellular Analyzer, which had originally been created by a young researcher, Mr. Ronald J. Weinstock, who lived in California. It was made not for measuring the quality of water, but to develop homeopathic remedies.*

Something struck me about the Bio Cellular Analyzer, so I promptly purchased three of them

---

*Homeopathy is a method of treatment established in the early 19th century by German doctor Samuel Hahnemann, and it's based on the idea that "like cures like." It uses the "one nail drives another" approach to cure by taking in a very small quantity of the substance that triggers the same response as the symptom of a sickness.

and brought them back to Japan. I then renamed the equipment the Magnetic Resonance Analyzer (MRA). At that time the MRA (Magnetic Resonance Angiography) that's presently used to scan blood vessels (among other things) had not yet been used and was unknown to me.

The equipment I brought back, however, was very difficult to operate. I was at that time managing an institution of acupuncture and moxibustion as an "antenna" shop for the sale of low-frequency therapy equipment, and I had several staff acupuncturists/moxa-cauterizers. However, none of them were able to use the MRAs for the purpose I intended. Soon they went to the storeroom to collect dust.

After a while, due to unforeseen circumstances, I lost the sales rights to the low-frequency therapy equipment, even though it was selling well, and was forced to close my shop. There was nothing left—except those three MRAs in the storeroom.

Almost in despair, I dragged the equipment out and tried to operate it following the "simple" manual provided by the developer. Being mechanically inept, I'd normally give up in 30 minutes, but this time I found myself absorbed by it for an entire hour. Before I knew it, two hours had passed.

I've always been terrible with machines and delicate manual work, but gifted with musical instruments. Without being taught by anyone, I have a special talent that allows me to play, albeit in my own way, various musical instruments, including the piano, violin, and trumpet. Once given a new instrument, I can play a scale after about half an hour. When I think back now, the MRA was like an unknown musical instrument for me. The key part of *magnetic resonance* is *resonance,* so the skill I needed was basically to distinguish different sounds.

Since then it's been as if I've gained an inner eye that allows me to measure the vibration of many things. This is how I leaned to measure water. In addition, the MRA has a function that measures the imbalance of vibrations within the body, and a function to copy the vibrations (hereafter called "HADO"*) in order to adjust them. I then chose the micro-cluster water that had been developed by Dr. Lorenzen as my medium.

The MRA had originally been developed, as stated earlier, for the purpose of homeopathy, and it was intended to be used with a 25 percent solution of alcohol. Homeopathy was not permitted in Japan at that time and it would have violated the Pharmaceutical Affairs Law and the Medical Act if an unlicenced person like me had given an alcohol solution to people. So it wasn't that I believed in or understood the ability of water to conduct information; it was just that my only choice was to use Dr. Lorenzen's water with the machine. Now I think it was just luck that there was no choice other than the water, or that at least I couldn't think of anything else. And it seems that my feelings toward water as my only hope invited the purity of energy.

While at the beginning I conducted the HADO measurements and created and offered HADO water in order to correct the distortions of HADO for the company staff, families, and relatives, I gradually realized that this technique implied a wonderful potential to deal with a blind spot of modern medicine (I'll go into HADO in more detail shortly). Word was passed on from person to person, and I went naturally along the path of alternative healer in the latter half of 1987.

After that, I worked to "cure illness" for about seven years. Having attempted various kinds of serious cases, I achieved remarkable results, which have been summarized in three published books: *Introduction to HADO Age* (Sunroad Publishing), *HADO Humanics* (Business-sha), and *HADO Sitology* (Takanawa Publishing).

When I published these books, my understanding of HADO had come a long way, and I had a lot of confidence in it. I went so far as to believe that without an understanding of the HADO way of thinking, there

x

---

*Although the developer would call it a "Magnetic Resonance Pattern," I use the Japanese word *HADO* (it rhymes with *shadow*), which literally means "wave" and "move," in order to make it easy to understand. HADO also means "wave motion" in physics, but this isn't how I'm using it in this text. You can think of HADO as "vibration."

could be no future. The public's reaction to these books, however, was that only specific people were interested in them, and most people didn't pay any attention to them at all. They certainly didn't sell well.

I kept wondering, *Why don't people see how important and simple it is?* The answer, I eventually realized, was that people don't believe what they can't see. With my spirit of defiance, I was determined to make HADO visible, and this resulted in the development of the current technique of frozen-water crystal photography. The ultimate purpose of my preparation of these pictures was to make invisible vibrations visible to us all.

## THE BIRTH OF FROZEN-WATER CRYSTAL PHOTOGRAPHY

It was the summer of 1994. I walked into a bookstore to kill time and ended up buying a book called *The Day That Lightning Chased the Housewife: And Other Mysteries of Science* by Julia Leigh and David Savold (HarperCollins). I opened the book and immediately noticed a sentence that said something to the effect of: "There are no two snowflakes that are alike." This was it! I thought, *Snow is frozen water. So if we freeze water, the water will be crystallized.* If we're able to take pictures of water before and after the HADO (vibration) is copied, and if we're able to display these pictures so that people can see how the crystals from the same water change, the world would become aware of, and accept the existence of, HADO. I remember feeling absolutely confident when I had this epiphany.

In the autumn of 1994, my plan began to take shape. After listening to me go on and on about my water-crystal idea for about two months, one of my staff members responded to my determination that we can take pictures of crystals. He was a decent scientist and a pure man who had completed his doctorate at a national university. He was new to my company, having just been hired in the spring of the same year.

This man worked hard through a continual process of trial and error for about two months. (Through this and later experiences, I've come to believe that purity is an absolute requirement for the people who study water.)

One day in September he ran into my office, his face beaming, holding a picture in his hand. "I got it, chief!" he announced. We shook hands firmly with each other. I still remember how deeply moved I was.

We continued taking pictures of frozen water crystals using various methods almost every day. The technique that shows letters and pictures to water was brought about from various experiences of HADO measurement, and the idea was nothing unconventional to me, so I adopted it naturally. These first pictures were compiled and published to the world as a photo album entitled *The Message from Water* (HADO Kyoikusha). It was June 1999.

More than a decade has passed since we started practicing water-crystal photography. The laboratory staff takes pictures of all kinds of water crystals every day in the large, cold refrigerators. As I mentioned in the Preface, what started with one researcher and one refrigerator has now become six researchers and three refrigerators. Today we take many more photos than ever before, and our results are much more stable. (For more technical details on how we collect specimens, photograph crystals, and analyze our results, please see the Appendix at the end of the book.)

The first crystal picture ever taken.

xi

## WHAT IS HADO?

Having managed to obtain the HADO measuring equipment and produce the HADO water, and having been able to cure a number of illnesses, I succeeded in the development of the technique of crystal photography, and since then I've been taking and observing pictures of various water crystals. As a result, I've come to firmly believe that the crystals themselves contain information in the form of vibrations.

After having experienced all that, I now believe that energy is created through vibrations. As I mentioned in the Preface, modern society seems lost in a maze of confusion. When you get lost, what should you do? Return to the starting point! But what is the starting point? It's our existence itself and the energy that created it. Then what is that energy?

Energy is vibrations, because everything is made of atoms, and the atoms vibrate in their nuclei. In organic matters, we can say the vibrations are life. For example, your heart is vibrating. When it stops vibrating, you'll be declared dead. That's why I think that in the middle of the Japanese character for the word *life,* 命, is found the character that means "to beat": 叩.

The problem is that the vibrations of organic matter can't keep moving automatically forever. To continue vibrating, they require the help of the third party. Resonance is the phenomenon that creates continuous vibrations. The resonance phenomenon has the following characteristics:

**The matching of frequencies creates a sympathetic vibration.** Take three tuning forks. Two are 440 hertz (abbreviated "Hz") and one is 442Hz. When we sound one of the 440Hz tuning forks, the other 440Hz tuning fork resonates fully, buzzing, but the 442Hz tuning fork resonates only slightly. We must listen for the sound of vibrations attentively. 440Hz is the "La" sound in the C major scale. When the 442Hz tuning fork is struck, it produces the same sound to our ears, but with only 2Hz difference, it doesn't resonate completely. As explained above, vibrations (energy) resonate only with the same frequency. The slightest frequency deviation reduces the possibility of resonance and eventually it stops vibrating.

This principle is used for radio frequencies. We used to select a radio station with a channel-selection dial. We succeeded in tuning when the frequency of the receiver in the radio and the frequency from the radio station matched. In addition, as radio has short- and medium-wave broadcasting capabilities, the length of the wave determines the distance of reach. Shorter wavelengths reach farther. In other words, the energy is stronger. Therefore, all international wireless communications and telephones are performed using short wavelengths.

When we strike the 440Hz tuning fork in the middle, only the left tuning fork, the one with the same frequency, resonates and makes a vibrating sound.

**Pure waves reach farther.** When waves become shortened, they can be seen as increasing in purity, because when the wave is short, interfering vibrations decrease. There is less space for disturbance. Therefore, the shorter wave can reach farther.

When we sit in Zen meditation, we're told to find a spiritual state of nothingness—a state that transcends self. This may mean that when we think about things in the normal course of our daily lives, gaps open up between the vibrations of our thoughts. This interferes with the creation of short waves, thus preventing our thoughts from reaching very far. I believe, therefore, that entering the state of nothingness is a HADO technology that allows us to come into contact with cosmic information.

Human beings have physical limitations regarding the range of sounds we can hear. That range goes from about 15Hz to 20,000Hz. To hear or transmit sounds far away, we have to use a frequency band exceeding the scope of our capability. In order to do this, we need something like a "communication box" that will carry information.

What allows us to accomplish this is water, and the molecular clusters in it. I believe that water circulates around the universe. Thus, by having an affinity to water, we can entrust our information to it. When the water reaches our counterpart, we can receive a message back from it through the echoing of resonance.

When the air surrounding the earth gets contaminated due to environmental pollution, the water also gets contaminated. We become lost children in the universe and get anxious that we're completely alone and living an unaided existence. But I believe that meditation may be developed and designed as one of various technologies to allow us, and thus our earth, to become pure. I published a book, *Awareness for the Universe and HADO* (PHP Institution, Inc.) in collaboration with Dr. Ravi Batra, an economist and master of meditation from India. On one occasion I saw him going into meditation. It was such wonderful art. Even though it was in a hotel room in the middle of a busy city, I felt that he was truly a man of unblemished character.

Let me tell you about an experiment some children performed to confirm the connection between HADO and purity. They prepared two bottles of cooked white rice with a label attached to each. One said "Thank You" and the other said "Idiot." They also repeated aloud to each bottle daily what the label said. One month later, the rice with the "Thank You" label had fermented to a yellow color, and the rice with "Idiot" had spoiled and gone black. I presented their results in *The Message from Water,* and many readers responded. They reported, with pictures, how they did the same types of experiments.

Almost all the responses we received were from children who had conducted similar tests. We received a few letters from adults, but in many cases their experiments didn't go as well—the outcomes were completely opposite or worked once but failed a second time. The thing is, children don't doubt. On the contrary, adults tend to be pessimistic, thinking, *What will I do if it doesn't turn out right?* or *It went well this time, but next time I need to do even better.* That is to say, they have a lack of purity about them. It's important not to doubt, and to just accept things as they are. This is key in the world of HADO.

One of my favorite responses came from a girl in elementary school who lived in Shimane Prefecture. For her experiment, she prepared containers of strawberries, oranges, and other fruit. She made several labels, which read: "Thank You," "Love," "Hello," "Ignored," and so on. She observed how they changed. Depending on the words, the fruit decayed differently. The samples with positive words took longer to go bad, and the samples with the negative words spoiled quickly. The reported results were wonderful.

Her comments from her experience were very moving, so I will share them with you: "If good words are created by good hearts, and good words change the water to make it possible to change the world for the better, then I'd like to start with what I can do to change the world for the better. I'd like to offer many "Thanks, I love you" calls from my heart to my father, mother, brothers, friends, and all the people I meet."

## PRAYERS AND WORDS CHANGE WATER AND CRYSTALS: FOUR CASE STUDIES

Now I'd like to introduce the results of experiments conducted under the theme of this book, which is prayer. There are photos of the crystals obtained in some of these experiments throughout the book.

## Study 1: Experiment with the Prayers of 500 HADO Instructors

The simple prayer of the HADO instructors changed the tap water to form beautiful crystals.

xiv

The first success of this experiment was on February 22, 1996. I put some tap water on the desk in my office in Tokyo and asked my fellow HADO instructors* all over Japan to say to the water the following sentence: "The water on the director's desk in Shinagawa, Tokyo, has become clean." That was all. I asked them to say this at two o'clock in the afternoon, and five minutes later, we froze the water. Three and a half hours later, the staff researcher came out from the refrigerator, muttering, "This can't be true!" You can see in the picture what we obtained after sending the sample out to develop right away. My fellow instructors had confidence in me, didn't they? That's why those words and wishes became pure HADO.

I was inspired to conduct this experiment by an experience I had at a "cloud-erasing game" that was taught by a friend of mine and was first started by Ms. Betty Shine from England. She discovered that when you say to the clouds in the sky, "The clouds have disappeared, thank you very much," in the past tense, the clouds disappear. I've erased the clouds before an audience many times, and I was even called the "Cloud-Erasing Game Man."

Of course I wondered why this worked, and my experience with curing many kinds of illness with the HADO water made me think that the vibrative aspect of words imparted some kind of physical effect to the clouds, which are made of water. Since it's possible, if the size is proper, to erase clouds in the distance easily, I asked my colleagues all over Japan to send words to the water in Tokyo, just as I had done in the cloud-erasing game.

## Study 2: The Dam-Water Purification Experiment

At the beginning of Chapter 4 in this book, I show the results of some experiments with water at the Fujiwara Dam in Japan. Basically, after praying over the water of the dam, we were able to obtain some absolutely breathtaking crystals. But there's more to this dam-water purification experiment: One week after we visited the dam, the office of the chief priest, Mr. Kato, informed us that a young woman's dead body had been found in the water near Fujiwara Dam. On the following day, the criminal who had killed the woman was arrested. Since we'd just been at the site, we were all shocked to hear this news. We reexamined the water crystal picture taken before the prayers, and guess what we found? An image that looked like a woman writhing in pain. Yes, much like spirit photography. I think it was because of the incantations and prayers of the chief priest that the body eventually surfaced.

The findings were incredible, but I could also interpret them in such a way that the spirit of the woman attained enlightenment. You see, in addition to the first crystal, I looked back on the other photos taken after the prayers, and there were some pictures of heptagonal crystals instead of hexagonal. Now I felt that I understood the meaning behind it. If hexagonal denotes a 3-dimensional world, then

*The purpose of HADO instructors is to convey the philosophy of HADO and its meaning beyond the boundaries of regions and nations. Having started with the first training in March 1994, more than 500 people have been registered as HADO instructors. We're not currently recruiting new instructors.

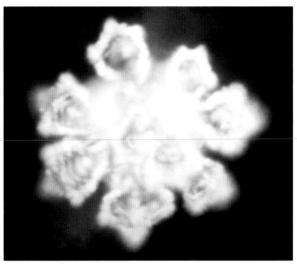

Can you see the image of the murdered woman in this crystal?

Does this heptagonal crystal reveal the enlightenment of the murdered woman?

heptagonal denotes the 3.5-dimensional world, which made me think that it must contain information from the world of sprits. I believe that water transcends dimensions and gives us information about other levels of existence. This conclusion is based on this experience.

Five years after this experience, I realized something very important about the water brought back from Lake Fujiwara. Both before and after the prayers, the typical dam water was obviously dirty. We could observe through the plastic bottle that it wasn't clear—it was polluted. I'd been questioning how we could obtain such beautiful, unearthly crystals from such filthy water.

That question was finally answered. The discovery was brought about by one incident: A Swiss woman made an absurd claim that she took the Fujiwara Dam crystal picture and announced this in her seminars and associated bulletins. This was in April 2003.

This irritation developed to the extent that I hired a local attorney and went to negotiate with the woman personally. The issue was finally settled, and she admitted that it was her fantasy and apologized. Because of this experience, I again wondered how we could have achieved such wonderful crystals from the

polluted water. I was also puzzled as to why someone would make the crazy claim that she took that picture. The woman who had done so was clearly not just after the publicity; in fact, she seemed very intelligent.

At this same time, I'd been advocating my theory as to why people get sick from the perspective of HADO theory, illustrating the difference in vibration level between elementary particles and atoms. Subsequently, when I seriously thought about the mystery again, I felt something click in my head, and a diagram came to me that provided clues to follow in order to solve this mystery.

xv

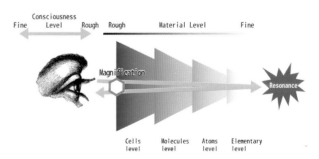

This is a diagram that describes the layers inside the human body. I believe that no matter how small pollutants and other trash are, they can only reach down to the atomic level. At the level of elementary particles, no matter how minute something is, as long as it has materiality, it can't enter. It's already a complete "World of HADO"—that is, "a world of senses and images."

But the chief priest's incantations and prayers reached that area of elementary particles and created a picture there. It played the role of drawing in the actual three-dimensional world beyond the atomic level. That's probably the reason why the dead body that had sunk to the bottom of the lake came to the surface after a time gap of approximately one week.

Mr. Masaya Sato, a staff member of the laboratory who shot the picture of the water, is an artist who has a pure heart. His mind's eye that seeks truth, virtue, and beauty went through the suspended substances and pollutants that normally block the view of the three-dimensional field on the cellular, molecular, and atomic level. He captured the picture that the chief priest drew. In other words, he resonated.

Resonance always accompanies the "echo phenomenon." The picture that Mr. Sato captured gave rise to the echo phenomenon, and it returned to his sight. Then it stayed at the molecular level as if it had always existed there. Mr. Sato caught that moment and released the shutter.

The Swiss woman who caused the disturbance might have, to some extent, had an ability similar to Mr. Sato's. From the moment when she first saw that crystal picture, the picture stayed in her mind. Without realizing it, she fell into the illusion that she took the picture herself.

If the above assessment is correct, we have made a big step toward understanding the essence of water. This means that human beings can start again any number of times, and that essentially there are no bad people. One could conclude that what can be freely drawn on the white canvas called the elementary particle level is the prayer of a pure person, and this makes the importance of prayer more clear.

## Study 3: The Experiment of Prayer at Lake Biwa

The next notable experience deserving special mention happened on July 25, 1999. It was the Lake Biwa purification experiment using the "Kotodama"—the power of words (there are photos of this event and the crystals we found in Chapter 4). Some 350 members gathered before sunrise that day at 4:30 A.M. I chose the date in accordance with the Mayan calendar, and the tradition that these ancient people prayed together at the crack of dawn.

That morning we all said the following: "The infinite power of the universe coalesced, took solid form, and created a truly harmonized world." It's a grand affirmation created by Tao Master Nobuo Shioya, who was 97 years old at that time. Under the direction of Master Shioya, who joined us eagerly in spite of his great age, we repeated the grand affirmation ten times. These words and wishes surely reached out to the universe. The story is already very famous, so I'm sure many people know about it, but I've included a summary of an article printed in a Kyoto newspaper on August 27 of that year.

Kyoto newspaper with the article on Lake Biwa.

A mysterious phenomenon is occurring in Lake Biwa this year. Usually at this time of year, we have an abrupt increase of algae of foreign origin that kills domestic algae due to the progress of the pollutant dioxin. This normally creates a foul odor, and over 300 phone-call complaints from the neighboring residents pour into the relevant offices every year. This year, however, there is no acrid smell; therefore no complaint calls were received. Although this is a very welcome phenomenon, it's not understood. The authorities concerned are trying to determine what's causing the change.

I was excited to see this article, since I wasn't expecting an outcome as spectacular as this. I reported this news to Master Shioya and, with composure, he told me that this was the obvious result. There is an infinite energy in the universe, and we said the great affirmation together to reach it. Then it created a true and great harmonious field around Lake Biwa. That's why the algae coexisted in harmony.

Was it the effect of ultrasonic waves? To be honest, at that time I felt unsure whether or not I truly understood what had happened. About eight months later, I finally got it after reading another newspaper article about dioxin, this time in a Sankei newspaper from April 16, 2000. Allow me to me paraphrase the article:

> A research team led by Professor Maeda of Osaka Prefecture University succeeded in the purification of lake and marsh water. They eliminated more than 95 percent of the dioxin and PCB in these lakes and marshes by running ultrasonic waves of 200,000 hertz to the water. The research team explained that when ultrasound waves are sent to water, countless bubbles are formed, and PCB and dioxin enter those bubbles because their nature has no affinity for water. Reacting to the stimulation, however, the bubbles soon explode. This releases heat—which reaches 5,000°C (more than 9,000°F)—causing PCB and dioxin to break down into their component nontoxic elements.

I think this article explains exactly what happened at Lake Biwa on that day in July when we prayed at the water. I believe the choral voice we made was vibrating near 300Hz. It was, in fact, very pure. This is because everyone who participated adores Master

Nobuo Shioya. In addition, it was dawn, so there were fewer interference vibrations in the environment. The vibrations were led by Kotodama, the power of words, and flew straight into the energy zone of the universe.

My belief is based on the idea of the octave theory (similar to the theory put forth in the Sankei newspaper), where each 600Hz; 1,200Hz; 2,400Hz; 4,800Hz; 9,600Hz; 19,200Hz; 38,400Hz; 76,800Hz; and 153,600Hz wavelength zones repeat their resonance and echo phenomenon and finally resonate with the frequency zone that resolves dioxin and PCB. We triggered the same phenomenon as the experiment at Osaka Prefecture University at Lake Biwa.

I'm confident that this idea will be widely accepted in the future, even though Kotodama (the power of words) is actually a religious phenomenon measured on a scientific scale.

### Study 4: The Experiment of Prayer from the Sea of Galilee to the Tap Water of Tokyo

Words and prayers transcend distance. I certainly came to believe this after a trip to the Sea of Galilee in Israel on July 25, 2003. This visit to Israel was for the Project Love and Thanks to Water, the purpose of which was to send love and thanks to the water of the world. I chose the River Jordan to hold an event with the support of the local people.

The experiment I was hoping to conduct was to send the words of prayer, or the power of words, from Israel to Japan and examine it with crystals. How far is it from Israel to Japan? It's probably about 10,000 kilometers (about 6,200 miles). To confirm beforehand the details of the experiment, I had a meeting with Mr. Kizu, who's in charge of the laboratory in Japan. The discussions centered around the time we would send the words of prayer, which words we'd send, and the preparation of slides so that the people in Israel could see where they were sending their words. We also discussed how to contact each other after the prayer, the amount of time it would take for Mr. Kizu to receive it, freeze the water, and take photos, and how to send the images captured back to Israel.

On the day of the experiment, I had a lecture scheduled at 11:00 A.M. local time. Three hours before I began, I asked the people attending the seminar to join me for a few minutes so we could conduct our experiment and have the results back from the lab in Japan in time for my talk. I had some photos prepared to illustrate exactly where the water was and where the people should send their prayers. Here's what I said to my audience of 200 that day:

> Ladies and gentlemen, thank you for coming today. I'd like to ask you to send to Japan a few words of prayer. Specifically speaking, I'd like you to send these words to the tap water that's standing in my office in Tokyo. First of all, please check where Japan is on the world map (picture 1). And this is Tokyo (picture 2). Here is my office and this is the entrance (picture 3). Can you visualize it now? My room is in here and I'm sitting, as you can see (picture 4). The water is right in front of me. This is the Tokyo tap water (picture 5). Usually the water is in this condition and it forms no crystals, because it contains a lot of chlorine for sterilization. Isn't that pathetic (picture 6)?

xviii

*Picture 2:* Tokyo, Japan.

*Picture 3:* The entrance to my office.

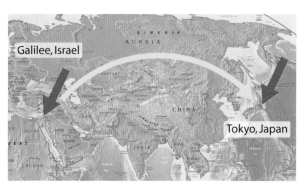

*Picture 1:* Israel to Japan.

*Picture 4:* Here I am at my desk with the tap water.

*Picture 5:* The Tokyo tap water.

*Picture 6:* Lack of crystals in the tap water.

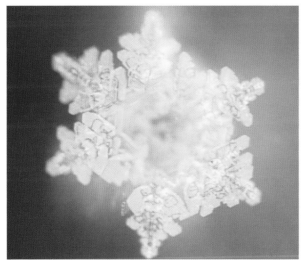

The prayer from Galilee reached the water in Tokyo.

Now, please send words of prayer to this water. It's late at night in Japan, but I have a member of my staff waiting for you to send these words. In three hours, he'll take a photo of whatever he finds in the water and e-mail it to me so I can show it to you. So please send prayers with all your heart. Repeat after me: *Water, we love you. Water, we thank you. Water, we respect you.* [I asked them to repeat this chant three times and then join me in one minute of meditation.] Thank you for your cooperation. I'll see you again at 11:00!

The picture Mr. Kizu would take was tentatively scheduled to be received by e-mail between 11:30 and noon. Pretending to be calm, I started my talk as usual. However, in my heart, I was beside myself with worry. Time passed. Before I knew it, I was worrying about what I'd do if no crystals were found. I kept glancing down at my computer. Finally, I received the e-mail. I announced to the audience: "The result of the Kotodama has apparently just now come. I'm also seeing this for the first time, so my heart is pounding."

The computer was already connected to the slide projector, so the image was immediately splashed on the screen in large scale. A stirring sound swept through the entire venue, then tremendous applause thundered. For a moment I was moved to tears.

I would never have dared to conduct a test like this on such a grand scale if I hadn't already had success with experiments such as the one with the 500 HADO instructors in the past. Because of the outcome of these events, I'm even more convinced of the power of prayer.

xix

## PUT YOUR HANDS
## TOGETHER AND PRAY

Sometimes it's rather difficult to pray "purely" in this complicated society. That's why I wrote a manual based on my many experiences with the pattern of prayer to water derived from the Project of Love and Thanks to Water. The manual states that we should make a circle holding hands with one another, put the water in the center of the circle, and chant together the following phrases: *Water, we love you. Water, we thank you. Water, we respect you.*

However, as I'll discuss in more detail in Chapter 1, I later realized that the most effective shape of prayer wasn't in holding hands, but in the form of praying hands—palms pressed together. We Japanese, in fact, were very accustomed to putting our hands together in the past. We still put our hands together from time to time, before and after meals and in front of the family Buddhist altar. This is also the way in which children apologize for being mischievous—and how they wish for a lot of New Year's presents.

In recent times, however, there are many people who feel hesitant to put their hands together, or who rarely do so because they feel it's too religious (although such people, in spite of themselves, make this gesture when something terrible happens—perhaps it's in our DNA). It's a pity. After witnessing the positive results of so many experiments based on this shape of prayer, and as a celebration of the publication of this book, I've decided to call out to my fellow global citizens: Let us pray by putting our hands together in the prayer position.

Once you're in the position to pray, there's one more thing I'd like to discuss, and that's the method of our prayer for world peace. It is, as I expressed in the Preface, to pray to yourself. Let me explain: There's a principle that nothing can continue vibrating all by itself. For example, when you spin a top, at the beginning it whirls vigorously, but soon it loses its force and comes to a halt. All kinds of engines or motors—including those in our cars—can't continue running without some type of fuel.

In the same way, no life can exist without water, because water delivers the energy that's called *vibration;* when the means of the energy supply is lost, no life form can survive. The 60 trillion cells of your body send a signal when their vibrations are becoming weak. It's expressed as the feeling of hunger, and therefore you eat. Each cell has a unique role, so each has a different vibration frequency. When the vibrations fade, your cells require the support of food with the same vibration frequency to create a resonance phenomenon and activate the cell again.

Junk food—in other words, food that doesn't have the required frequency level—disturbs the vitality of cells. It's the same as being around someone with whom you don't get along; you get stressed and lose energy. When you pray for world peace on behalf of someone other than yourself, what you're really doing is sending good vibrations to other people. To do this, you yourself need to be vibrating in good health. And for that reason, you need to be well and happy. This is the basis of everything, the beginning of it all.

It's only when you like who you are, feel grateful for your existence, and respect yourself that you're able to have the same feelings toward other people. The nature of vibrations is such that negative resonates only with negative and positive resonates only with positive. No matter how much you say and think good things, you can't give off good vibrations as long as you have a distorted image of your substance.

When we shine and keep sending out positive vibrations, they reach the people and the water around us, and eventually they spread like ripples all over the world. It reminds me of when I was a child and I used to see all the flotsam and jetsam from distant countries that had reached the shores of Tokyo Bay. As proved in the experiment at a lake in Carapicuiba (Chapter 4), when the group of less than 20 sent the prayer of love and thanks to the small amount of water taken from the lake, the vibrations spread all over the lake. The pure prayer to the small amount of water was capable of conveying the same vibrations to the surrounding water. Indeed, we shouldn't forget that we ourselves are water.

I've been studying why people get sick, from the point of view of HADO, for about 15 years. It's clear that illness is primarily caused by distortions of vibrations at the level of elementary particles. Think of it this way: If the planet Earth, or the entire human race, is a person, then each one of us is an elementary particle. The distortions of each individual will grow to become the disease of the entire world.

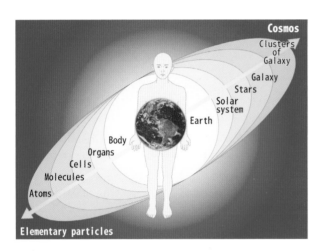

If you accept this idea, even if you don't fully understand it, pray for yourself from today in the following manner. I'm sure something will change within you. Here's how to do it.

- **Time/Place:** You can pray anytime and any-where: when you wake up, before you go to sleep, when you're taking a walk, before a meal, or anytime you're spending a quiet moment alone.

- **Feelings/Image:** Try to recall feelings of thanks to the water. Picture all the people in the world holding hands with one another in harmony; and our water planet, Earth; and the water of our bodies.

- **The Three Phrases:** Say to yourself: *[Your name] I love you. [Your name] I thank you. [Your name] I respect you.* If it's difficult to say aloud, say it in your heart first. You'll get used to it. After this, it's also a good idea to say the name of a person who you're concerned about or who is on a different wavelength.

- **Posture:** Close your eyes and put your hands together.

It's very easy, isn't it? Each prayer lasts only 30 seconds. And of course it's no problem if you want to take a little longer.

When you start praying, something will definitely transform within you. And when more and more of your fellow humans evolve in the same way, your surroundings will change, society will change, the country will change, and the world will change . . . all in a good direction, of course.

✳✳✳ ✳✳✳

# CHAPTER ONE

## The Shape of Prayer

*When praying with the palms together, the people were filled with spiritual feelings.*

My grandson, who grew up knowing instinctively to put his palms together.

When Japanese are asked to draw "the shape of prayer," I think every one of us would sketch the shape of two palms pressed together. People from other countries would probably design similar images, although they may vary slightly depending on the social climate and the religion.

But why is putting the hands together connected to prayer? And why is this such a common practice all over the globe? Customs don't become such by accident. There must be a compelling reason behind the tradition.

I realized this myself when I reached the idea that energy means *vibrations,* and vibrations continue by resonance. In other words, energy isn't generated independently.

The right hand alone can't create an energy current. Only with the left hand added is a smooth circulation created. And I realized that ancient people, perhaps to receive the energy of the sunlight, opened their hand widely, and when they sent this energy to others as prayer, they quietly closed their eyes and prayed with both hands together in order for their emotional energy to be transmitted purely.

In this section, I'll introduce crystal pictures that happen to contain the shape of praying hands from our experiments under the theme of prayer. Were these just coincidence, or did they appear as they did because they should have? What do you think?

✦ ✦ ✦

3

# Wa (Harmony)

We showed the word *Wa* written by both a calligrapher and a word processor to separate containers of distilled water. Both formed the crystal of the "shape of prayer." However, the formation created in the sample that was shown the calligraphy was clearer. It seems that the soul of the calligrapher can have a strong influence on the crystals.

Japan was once called the "Country of Wa," or "Country of Yamato," meaning "Great Harmony"). I believe a spiritual awareness existed that attempted to raise the people's consciousness to pray for harmony in all things. I think it's important to never forget that—no matter how much time has passed. Indeed, "Harmony is the greatest of virtues."

4

## Gregorian Chant

This is a crystal we found in the water that we'd played a Gregorian chant to. Considered one of the foundations of classical Western music, Gregorian chant has been sung for more than a thousand years as liturgical music in the Catholic Church. The center of this crystal looks like a mouth singing with all its soul, and the prayer is concentrated in one point in the heavens.

## "Amazing Grace"

This is a crystal of water exposed to the sound of "Amazing Grace." The words of this famous hymn were written by John Newton, the former master of a slave ship who had a change of heart when he miraculously survived a violent storm at sea. Later he atoned for his sins and became a minister in the Church of England. In this crystal, both heaven and earth appear in the typical shape of prayer.

6

## Amen

We showed the word *amen,* written in Japanese, to a sample of water. *Amen* is from Hebrew originally, but it's now used universally with Christianity. It's a confirmation that "what we have just said is true" at the end of every prayer and choral hymn. To me, it sounds like the word of prayer itself.

# Fish Symbol

Early Christians used the symbol of a fish to represent Christ. This is said to be due to the fact that *Ichthys,* the Greek word for "fish," is an acrostic for "Iesous Christos Theou Yios Soter," or "Jesus Christ, Son of God, Savior." It's an interesting coincidence that the first four disciples of Christ were fishermen.

## Gassho (Hands Joined in Prayer)

Exposed to the word *Gassho,* the shape of prayer in the crystal stretched out in all directions (left). Maybe the feeling of true hope was reached because later it grew to become an absolutely gorgeous crystal, as you can see in the picture on the right. Looking at it carefully, it almost resembles the face of Ryujin, the Dragon God of Water.

10

# Heitate Shrine

This is a crystal from water exposed to the picture of the Heitate Shrine in the town of Soyo, Kumamoto Prefecture, in Kyushu. It's said to date back 15,000 years, and it's where the Takamagahara myth supposedly originated. The shrine is dedicated to Amaterasu Omikami, the Sun Goddess. This is the first crystal picture that made me fully aware of the shape of prayer.

# Jehovah

Jehovah is the God of Judaism and is regarded as the creator of all nature and the supreme ruler of the universe. This is a picture of a water crystal exposed to the Hebrew letters that spell "Jehovah." This formation closely resembles the crystal of the Heitate Shrine picture. Some scholars of history suggest that the ancient Yamato people (Japanese) and the ancient Jewish people were closely related, like brothers. However, this is most certainly a very controversial theory.

## Nanboku Toitsu (Unification of North and South)

We showed these words, written in Korean, to the water. Judging by the results, I truly believe that this phrase expresses the deep desire for the unification of North and South Korea. It may be a more accurate reflection of the thoughts and sentiments of the South Korean people, because we asked our Korean publishing company to choose "Unification of North and South" for the theme of the Korean version of *The Message from Water*. Is that the reason why the prayer is directed due north?

13

## Kyomei (Resonance)

We showed the word *resonance* to the water. Perhaps the source of resonance can be found within heaven. All things seem to be receiving that resonance, holding hands and harmonizing. I believe Nirichin (the sun) is at the center of the crystal.

# CHAPTER TWO

## A Cornucopia of Prayer

*Religious words, prayers, and music are all wonderful.*

My grandson, coming home from the hospital to meet our cat for the first time.

This chapter offers a random selection of the crystals we found when we showed and played words and phrases, music, and pictures related to prayer to the water. I'd like to ask that you try to feel something as you look at the various images. I'll tell you what emotions and thoughts the photos elicited in me, but only as an example. What you experience is what the water intends to tell you.

16

# Han-nya-shin-gyo (Heart Sutra)

This is a water crystal produced from the 266 characters of the Han-nya-shin-gyo, or Heart Sutra, which is a Buddhist scripture from ancient India. This sutra, full of esoteric wisdom, is the most widely known among the Japanese, and it's recited and transcribed in almost all denominations of Japanese Buddhism.

I have a feeling that the seventh chakra of the seven chakras,* the parietal lobe, has been activated. It's supposed to be your link to oneness with the entire cosmos.

*People have seven vital energy centers, called *chakras,* related to the mind and body, starting from the first one at the bottom of the spine to the seventh at the parietal lobe.

# Shiki-soku-ze-ku Ku-soku-ze-shiki

*Shiki-soku-ze-ku* is a phrase within the Han-nya-shin-gyo (Heart Sutra) that means "existence is without form." *Ku-soku-ze-shiki* means "formless *is* existence," and each existence has meaning, and in a sense, is shining.

I interpret this phrase as being associated with quantum mechanics. It's a wonderful expression of the physical phenomenon of the quantum world, where everything switches on and off at extreme speed. I think that the dark hollow you can see in the middle of the crystal is *Ku*, or emptiness, and the beautiful branches are *Shiki,* form.

18

# Namu-myoho-renge-kyo

We showed the phrase *Namu-myoho-renge-kyo* to the water. Nichiren, a Buddhist of the Kamakura period (about 800 years ago), was the first to chant these words. They express the believer's desire to call upon the Lotus Sutra for help and protection. Nichiren taught that one should repeatedly chant this sutra un-self-consciously.

Even if we don't know the exact meaning of the phrase, this is certainly a beautiful crystal that makes us want to keep it close to us at all times.

## Namu-amida-butsu

This is a chant recited by the Pure Land sect of Buddhism (Jodu-shu), which was established by Honen at the end of the Heian period (more than 800 years ago). It means "to become a devotee of the Buddha Amida." It's also known as the *nenbutsu,* or invocation.

In the photo of the crystal, the light stretching toward the inner core from each of the six bottom corners is like a tuning fork. The recipient, in the center, is colored pink and green. In my HADO theory, pink is love and green is thanks.

20

# Amaterasu Omikami (Sun Goddess)

We showed the words *Amaterasu Omikami* to the water. *Amaterasu Omikami* means "Goddess of the Sun," and this deity was once regarded as the central figure in the Japanese pantheon. The name appears in the Chronicles of Classical Japan, and according to the Kojiki ("The Record of Ancient Matters"), it was revealed when Izanagino Makoto washed his left eye in a purification ceremony.

I was most surprised when I saw this crystal. First of all, many people my age are worried that conducting an experiment such as this is akin to blasphemy. But after viewing the results, I came to a sense of confidence and awe. The second photograph shows that the crystal expanded as the temperature rose. It really looks just like the Sacred Mirror, one of Three Sacred Treasures of Shin-to.

21

## Happy Christmas (English)

The English greeting "Happy Christmas" possesses
a noble beauty, like that of an English gentleman. It
has a feeling of seeking happiness within beauty.

22

## <u>Happy Christmas (Italian)</u>

It varies depending on the language, doesn't it? *Felice Natale*—this crystal looks like the very definition of merrymaking and holiday cheer. Doesn't that sound Italian?

## Taizoukai Mandala

The Taizoukai is one of the mandalas for Shingon esoteric Buddhism. It's based on a comment in the Dainichikyo, a Buddhist sutra. I still don't know what it means. However, the crystal from the water exposed to the picture of the Taizoukai Mandala looks very similar to the crystal I grew after showing the word *mother* (see small photo). It's full of mercy that wraps around you gently. It also looks like the picture of birth—of new life coming from the central hollow.

24

## <u>Kongoukai Mandala</u>

This mandala is one of wisdom and insight. Its meaning is perhaps most closely translated as "out of the counsel of three comes wisdom." It's based on the Kongochokyo, a Buddhist sutra. Since it's divided into nine parts, it's also called the *Kue Mandala (Kue* meaning "nine"). I feel instinctively that it will form a complete whole if combined with the Taizoukai Mandala.

# InYo (Yin and Yang)

The fundamental principal of the universe in Eastern philosophy is *InYo* (yin and yang). All materials and phenomena arise from two types of *qi* (energy), *In* (yin) and *Yo* (yang), and exist in relative relations of the two. The interpretation of InYo principles is very difficult, but I think the key point with it lies with the small *In* within the large *Yo*, and the small *Yo* within the large *In*. The water crystal exposed to the characters of InYo turned out very close to that meaning.

26

# Islam 99 Words

We showed the water the 19th word of the 99 Islam words. The meaning of the word is "a person of wisdom." We then obtained this gorgeous crystal.

# Cross

We showed only a simple cross to the water, but it
formed this profound crystal.

28

## Basmalah

Basmalah is a very important sutra passage for Muslims. It's recited before doing many activities, such as eating a meal, going to bed, and so forth. The water exposed to Basmalah crystallized as an impeccably beautiful crystal. It bears a close resemblance to the crystal of Neighborly Love on page 70.

"Change"

"Truth"

"Change"

"Truth"

## Pictures of Babaji "Change" and "Truth"

While in fact I hadn't heard of Babaji until recently, I received many questions about him during my seminars in Europe. Upon further investigation, I learned that he is a holy man said to have been born in India in the third century. Some claim that he's immortal, and he's supposedly still alive and about 1,800 years old. A person who believes in Babaji lent me a book of paintings he made, and I brought it back to Japan and had my staff photograph it. After showing the photos to water samples, we achieved a series of beautiful hexagonal crystals. What do you think of these?

32

## <u>Star of David</u>

There's no doubt that this symbol is a geometric pattern that creates positive energy, because this picture was taken by a trainee who's going to enter our company in the near future. Two triangles have to become one in order to resonate and create this three-dimensional energy. At least that's what I think.

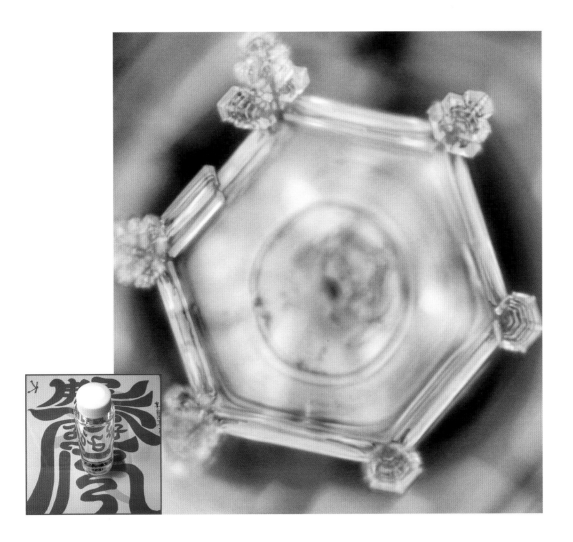

## Kyureifu

An acquaintance of mine brought this painting to me. This particular talisman was developed in Taoism in order to have prayers granted by the immortals. It's regarded as the reflection of the aura of the natural world and the power of the immortals. And indeed, the crystal turned out to be structured like a soul being protected. Might the large crystal behind the smaller one be a background spirit?

34

A European fountain decorated with Christian images.

# Christianity

It looks like six gorgeous Christmas trees have formed simultaneously, and each one is exquisitely beautiful.

36

# Buddhism

The crystals that were achieved by showing water the word *Buddhism* had hollow cores. Buddhism recognizes the Other World. Is the hollow a connection to that place?

## Judaism

This formation has a beautiful overlapping structure. The background crystal is a large one, which also has the shape of prayer. It's pouring out energy.

## Islam

The central pillar is shining rainbow colors, while
each branch tip extends powerfully upward, just like
the crystals of the other religions.

## Hinduism

This crystal has a pleasing, gentle, and round look,
overall. There are various denominations of Hinduism,
but this crystal gives the impression of unification.

Buddhism, Christianity, Judaism,
Islam, and Hinduism.

## Five Religions

We obtained an astonishing result when we showed the names of five religions—Buddhism, Christianity, Judaism, Islam, and Hinduism—to a sample of water. What appeared at the top of the crystal looks to me like the deity within every one of us! All five religions are wonderful, but even more spectacular may be the message that's being conveyed by this crystal.

## 666

We showed the number 666, which appears in the Bible's Book of Revelation as the number of the "beast," to a sample of water. In general, it created only dirty crystals. However, I dared to select this photo to publish because I think that depending on the way you look at it, there's something attractive about it—just as it's said that evil can be glamorous.

42

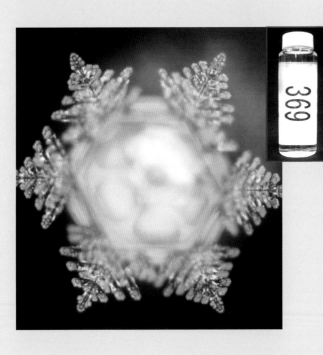

## 369

The number 369 is regarded as the opposite of 666. Subtracting 369 from 666 in each column makes 6-3 = 3, 6-6 = 0, and 6-9 = -3. These totals, when added together, make 0, which is symbolic of the annihilation of evil phenomena. Some people say that the Japanese Buddha of the future, the Miroku Bosatsu, is derived from this number (*mi-ro-ku* sounds similar to *three-six-nine* in Japanese). Indeed, as you can see, the crystal is very beautiful, and in the center you can see a face like that of Daikoku, God of Fortune.

## 666/369

When we showed both 666 and 369 to a sample of water at the same time, the result was a beautiful twin-shaped formation. It may be possible that the Miroku Bosatsu (Japanese Buddha of the future) legend is correct. This is good news for people who have been fearful of the number 666.

44

# Shomyo

Simply put, *Shomyo* is a chorus of sutra chanted by priests for memorial services. We played for the water a Shomyo called "Scattering Flowers" that's traditionally sung while sprinkling lotus petals. As expected, the crystals appear in a series, like the petals of a flower. Would it be possible to ascend to heaven if led by this Shomyo?

## "Kimigayo" (Japanese National Anthem)

The distilled water that had been exposed to the sound of "Kimigayo" (with the lyrics) formed this beautiful crystal. It is, however, also a fact that some people are reminded of an unpleasant past when they listen to this song. The water in such people's bodies may naturally form different crystals.

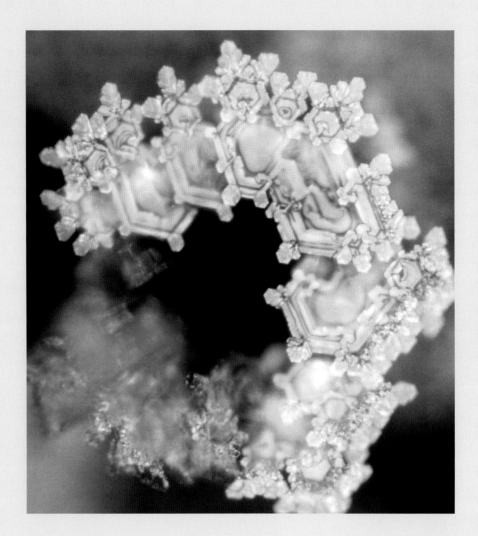

46

## "Ave Maria"

This is a crystal produced by playing "Ave Maria," written by Charles Gounod and Johann Sebastian Bach and sung by Susan Osborn. It was recently used as the theme music of a Japanese film called *Gaia Symphony*. When Ms. Osborn came to our office and we showed her this photograph, she was so moved that she burst into tears. She said that the crystal precisely expresses the feelings she has when she sings this song. It certainly seems to stir our souls.

## "Silent Night"

In the center of this formation appeared a truly beautiful pearl. When we listen to this song, it feels as though our souls are being cleansed.

48

## "Imagine"

This is the crystal exposed to the song "Imagine" by John Lennon. Like the words of this song, it's a beautiful and unique crystal where each individual grows freely and with perfect harmony. I've included the lyrics of the song here because they seem almost like a prayer.

Imagine there's no heaven
It's easy if you try
No hell below us
Above us only sky
Imagine all the people
Living for today

Imagine there's no countries
It isn't hard to do
Nothing to kill or die for
And no religion, too
Imagine all the people
Living life in peace

Imagine no possessions
I wonder if you can
No need for greed or hunger
A brotherhood of man
Imagine all the people
Sharing all the world

You may say I'm a dreamer
But I'm not the only one
I hope someday you'll join us
And the world will be as one

50

## The Koran

We played the water an audiotape of the Koran. It was sung in the traditional manner—deeply and richly without musical accompaniment. The resulting crystal turned out to have a very symbolic form.

## Masugata Pond at the Kokubunji, Tokyo

Kokubunji is a commuter town in the Tokyo megalopolis. Normally we wouldn't expect to see pond water in the middle of such a town make a crystal a beautiful as this, since the water would inevitably be contaminated by various kinds of domestic pollution.

But actually, I drew this water from the pond myself. The park surrounding the pond has good HADO, and many people were relaxing there. In addition, it was landscaped very well to allow good communication with the water.

52

## <u>Spring Water of Tamaki Shrine, Kumano</u>

This is a crystal picture of the spring water in Tamaki Shrine, known as the Inner Sanctum of Kumano. It's situated immediately beneath the top of the Tamaki mountain in Totsugawa Village, Wakayama, and it's dedicated to the god Kunitokotachino Mikoto.

The crystal itself has a unique shape with five layers—what is it telling us? With further investigation, I believe that the various mysteries will be revealed. Conducting these studies isn't just dry research—it's a very enjoyable occupation.

## Miracle Spring in Naju, Korea

This water was brought to us from Korea. We were told that the water is known as the Korean "Spring of Lourdes" because a woman who lived in Naju was directed by the Virgin Mary to dig in a specific location. When she did so, water gushed out. To this day, pilgrims flock to the spring to experience its healing powers.

The man who brought us the water from Naju had been an elite engineer from a prestigious company. He was also a devout Christian, and when he saw the water crystal we photographed, he decided to leave his job to pursue spiritual endeavors. It's not unusual for a single water crystal to change a person's destiny. It certainly happened in my case!

54

## Zamzam, Saudi Arabia

This is a crystal of the sacred spring water near Jetta in Saudi Arabia. It was brought to us by an Arab person living in Japan, with whom I'd had a chance to get acquainted. The raw water has many particles, so we diluted it to 1/1000th with distilled water. This beautiful water from the desert turned out crystals with overlapping forms every time—it was mystifying.

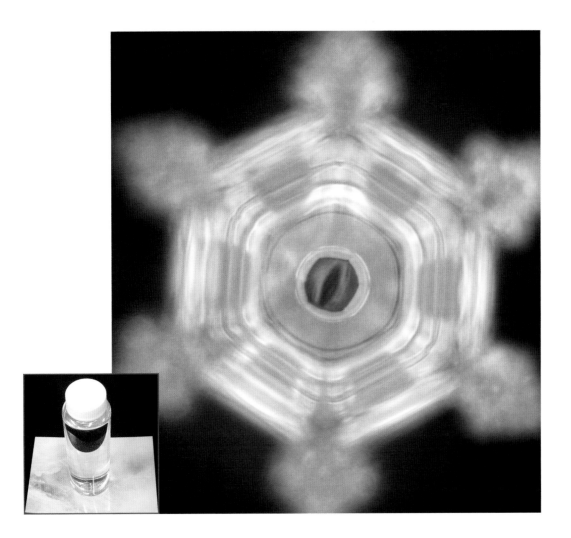

## Niagara Falls, United States of America

The ascetic practice of sitting under a cold waterfall provides the most effective mental training. It's said that the basin beneath a waterfall is full of negative ions and positive *qi* (energy). The crystal we received substantiated this theory. Its core looks like the eye of a dragon.

## Mecca, Saudi Arabia

We showed a picture of the sacred Muslim city of Mecca to a sample of water. We also tried our experiment with several other photos of the city, but we chose to print this one because surprisingly, the crystal came out looking exactly like a particular aerial shot we'd used.

## Sukato Temple, Thailand: Rainwater from Three Jars

We performed an experiment to investigate the relationship between places of healing and crystals. We checked crystals of rainwater contained in jars and placed in the Wa Pa Sukato Temple in Thailand (a temple for meditation), the forest surrounding the temple, and a village a little ways away from the temple. The water was collected during the rainy season. Depending on where the jars were kept, the water crystals showed puzzling differences in maturity.

58

# *Rainwater from the Jar in the Village*

Since the jar was in a place where it's constantly affected by the emotions of villagers, this restlessness may have influenced the water. Among the three samples, the least number of beautiful crystals was found in this jar.

 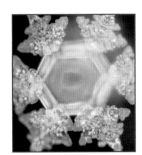  

# *Rainwater from the Jar in the Forest*

Perhaps because it was the place with the least human activity, the rhythms of nature nourished the rainwater. We were successful in obtaining more beautiful crystals in this sample compared to the water left in the village.

60

## *Rainwater from the Jar in the Temple*

The priest and villagers meditate in the Sukato Temple daily. A healing space has been created through the consciousness of the people. Out of the three samples, we observed the greatest number of beautiful crystals in the water left in the temple.

## <u>Elephant</u>

We showed pictures of elephants to the water and then photographed the results. This crystal is typical of those that formed. What's amazing is that you can see the trunk of an elephant in the center of the crystal.

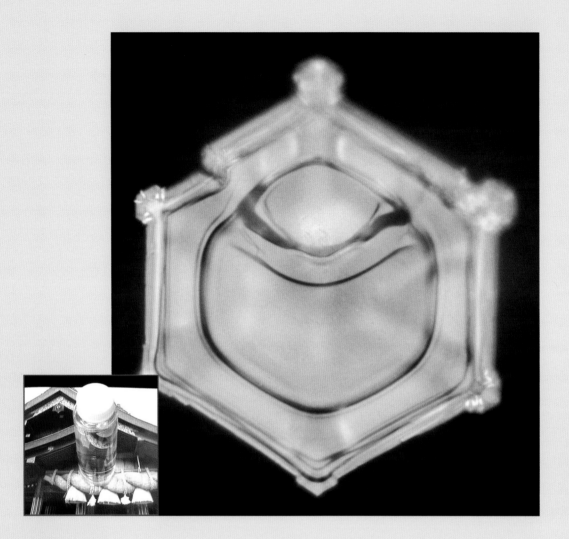

## Izumo Shrine

In this picture, the shapes of the Izumo Shrine's sacred straw ropes and the top of the shrine itself are clearly visible within the crystal. This result leads me to wonder if perhaps vibrations that are associated with images or shapes could remain in the brain in that form. This might be a clue to help us solve the mechanism of "thought photographs" and memory.

## Giant Camphor in Kawako

The exact shape of the complicated roots of a giant
camphor tree appear in the form of this crystal.

## Heart

We showed the water a heart shape, and the water formed an identical crystal. What's also incredible about this formation is that resembles the Japanese character 心 (Koroko), which means "heart." To some, this crystal is a little crooked, and it looks like a heart splitting into two pieces. Water crystals can really be a great deal of fun!

# CHAPTER THREE

## The Power of Words

*"In the beginning, there was the Word . . ."*

Baby and kitty conversing with each other?

Words themselves are energy. In my seminars, I always stress that energy is vibration, and vibration is life. I follow this by saying that words are vibrations. Syllogistically speaking, therefore, words are life!

In archaic Japanese, a written character 命 *(Inochi, meaning "life")* was pronounced "Mikoto," which meant "Mikotoba"—or holy words. It might be that words were considered "Inochi," life.

Archaic Japanese words were used during the time when ancient Shin-to was the main culture. I don't mean Shin-to in the sense of a religion or cult. While today the characters 神 道 are pronounced "Shin-to," I believe that in the past they were pronounced "Shin-do," which means "the way of the gods." In other words, I believe that 振動 (read "Shin-do," meaning "vibrations") was the original meaning of 神道 ("Shin-do,"meaning "the way of the gods"). That means that the ancient Japanese, or Yamato ("Great Harmony") people knew that everything begins with vibrations. I believe that they were aware that vibrations are life, light, and sound, and this knowledge led them to a higher existence—perhaps they were the gods themselves. Maybe they knew everything about what is now called *quantum mechanics.*

The answer to the question, "Why do water crystals change depending on words?" is *vibration.* After all, how did words begin? Here's my theory: Your parents, who raised you, taught you words. Words aren't contained in your DNA. So how did the first human beings learn

65

words? I think they picked them up from the vibrations in nature, of which sounds are made.

Various sounds can be heard in nature: safe, dangerous, quiet, noisy, pleasant, unpleasant, soothing, unsettling, strange, familiar, and so forth. I think people created words for the purpose of distinguishing these sounds and sharing them with others. So the sounds of words are nothing less than a divine gift from nature. Water crystals illustrate this gift in their design. Negative things prevent the water from crystalizing, while that which is positive develops beautiful hexagonal shapes.

This way of thinking provides a good reason for the differences in words around the world. Each country has its own unique natural environment. The vibrations in nature, which are the basis of words, vary. Thus, words differ depending on the climate rather than the country. However, the gift of nature is the same everywhere, so although words may be different, their meaning is the same.

Water is a medium that receives and understands even the subtlest vibrations. Water captures vibrations naturally—even when they're written in characters or letters representing language—and shows us the energy they contain in the form of crystals.

Words most certainly have power. In this chapter I'll show you the results of a number of experiments with positive words, and a few experiments with negative ones. I'd like you to remember a time when you encountered these words personally, and please feel, once again, the meaning and forces behind them.

67

## Jikoai (Self-Love)

We showed the word *Jikoai,* meaning "self-love," to the water. If we're unable to love ourselves, we can't truly love others. We must be shining—in other words, our vibrations should be full of energy; otherwise, we can't resonate with others. The water seems to be saying, "First resonate and vibrate from the inside; clasp your hands within yourself."

## Fufuai (Wedded Love)

Can't we really love our partner only when we
truly love ourselves? When we do, our affection grows
into a tender, caring love.

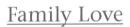

69

## Family Love

Once it was common for three generations to live together as a family. In recent times, this has become difficult because of housing conditions and declining birth rates. This is creating various problems. When we showed the phrase "Family Love," the crystal grew into three layers. I interpret this as follows: The bottom layer represents the grandparents, the middle layer is the parents, and the top layer is the children. It gives the impression that the presence of grandparents is the most important factor.

70

# <u>Neighborly Love</u>

Jesus said, "Love thy neighbor." Likewise, there's a saying in Japanese that goes: "Three neighbors across, and one on each side." Both phrases means the same thing—that we must help one another. There seem to be many people nowadays who have no contact with their neighbors. Let's take the time to think of those around us once again as we look at this crystal.

## Patriotism

The large, hazy crystal in the background may represent one's homeland. I don't give much thought to my country when I'm at home, but I think about it a lot when I'm abroad. I feel proud to be Japanese, and I tend to seek out people who feel the same way.

Some might say that we need to grow beyond simple patriotism in order to achieve true globalization. However, I believe that we can only understand and love one another when we know and love ourselves.

72

## <u>Love for Humanity</u>

This crystal greatly resembles the one from "Neighborly Love." It truly expresses the idea that you see a part to see the whole, and you see the whole to see a part, doesn't it? First you must be able to love yourself, and then you'll be able to love your family. Only then can you love your neighbors, and from there, your homeland and humankind.

## Reverence

We can really see the shape of love and respect in this crystal. Whenever I see a person I revere, I unconsciously assume an attitude of respect and find myself full of love and honor for his or her very existence. Please imagine a person you respect and love. I'm sure you'll have feelings that resemble this crystal.

74

## Kando (Emotion)

The word 感動 (Kando) is a reverence of vibrations. Kando means "to feel" or "to be moved." To be affected by strong emotion and vibrate is the best energy source (it's energy and motion). The more Kando you have every day, the more energetic your life will be. Again, the crystals that were created from the word *Kando*, or *emotion,* have the shape of prayer.

When you happen to encounter something you've been hoping and praying for, you feel a thrill. This should give you a clue as to how to live a vibrant life. I believe that having a lot of positive desires and praying for them is the key to living a richly emotional life.

## Hope

This is the crystal for "Hope." We actually wanted to show this through video, because if you could see the six well-balanced branches grow, you'd definitely feel that having hope is wonderful. In addition, when crystals grow and thrive in this manner, their core is strongly constructed. Only when provided with a solid foundation can great hope thrive.

## Peace

We showed the word *Peace* to the water. A crystal
that looked like a fusion of the crystals of "Love and
Thanks" (see Chapter 4) appeared.

## <u>War</u>

We showed the word *War* to the water. Smashing through the crystal of "peace," here is a formation resembling the moment the jet airliners crashed into the World Trade Center on September 11. This picture was taken in July of the same year. It's almost as if water has predictive abilities.

# Despair

As expected, most crystals developed timidly and turned out pitiful. On the other hand, there were two crystals similar to this one that didn't quite form a hexagon. We can feel their desire to work vigorously to recover and grow into things of beauty. Let's realize that despair may be the start of new hope!

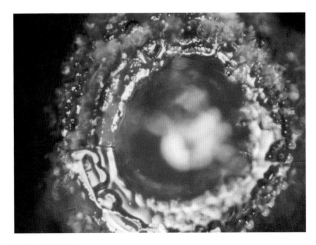

## Blasphemy

Blasphemy is a contemptuous or profane act, utterance, or writing concerning God or a sacred entity. When you look at the composition of the character carefully, 涜, you can see that it's made of symbols meaning "water" and "to sell," giving us the meaning "to sell water." This supports my hypothesis that water may be a messenger of God. When this occurred to me for the first time, I actually got goose bumps.

Throughout recent history, we've seriously polluted our water. This explains why we have to buy and sell this natural resource. Reflecting on this for the future, I'd like us to be able to live in a world where water is something we all respect and share.

It's also interesting that regardless of whether we used the Japanese or English language to spell "Blasphemy," we obtained the same type of crystals.

# Human Cloning

The water firmly said no to these words. It's probably because it's not natural. In addition, there appears to be a strange code on something that looks like a slate in the middle of the crystal. What does this mean? Is it some sort of identification?

## Truth

This crystal has perfect symmetry. Many people say that in geometry lies truth, and this shape actually gives me that impression. It's a formation that beckons us to admire it all the time . . . perhaps even keep it on our desk.

82

## Honesty

Be honest with your own heart. Never tell a lie,
and cultivate your true self. Then, one day, your heart
will be a shining gem like this crystal.

## Happiness

What is true happiness? Is it possible for you alone to be happy? Or for just your family to be happy? What about only your country or your planet? No, this is impossible, because I like to believe that happiness, "shiawase" in Japanese, is the same as the phrase "shi-a-wa-se," which describes water that is calm and peaceful in all four directions.

If surrounded by "happy" water, trees and flowers will be full of life and will clothe themselves in green, giving forth fresh, clean air for us to breathe. In turn, a world is created that allows all living things to exist in harmony. So how can we be sure that we're surrounded by happy water?

How about asking the composer of the universe? Indeed, the cosmos is said to have begun with "1," and "1" also symbolizes each of us. So let us all be happy first! And of course to do that, we must love ourselves.

84

## Eternity

This crystal also possesses perfect symmetry, and at first glance it appears to have an overlapping structure. The photographer focused on the outermost part of the crystal, leaving the inner portion somewhat blurry.

I believe that if we'd been able to focus on the entire formation at once, we'd have seen a never-ending series of crystals of the same shape within the core.

## Hemp

Hemp, or cannabis, has been grown naturally since ancient times. Due to the fact that hemp rope and marijuana come from the same plant, its cultivation is currently against the law in most of the world. We showed the word *Hemp* to one sample of water and a picture of the plant to another sample. In my opinion, the water crystals replied in the affirmative for society's use of hemp.

# CHAPTER FOUR

## The Power of Prayer

*If the people of the world prayed to water . . .*

You and I are also brothers!

Many people know of the Apollo 13 space launch in April of 1970 and its miraculous return to Earth. The movie *Apollo 13* that was released several years ago revived this event for a new generation. The element of the story that intrigues us to this day is how these astronauts made it back home when there was so little chance of success.

I was 27 years old at the time of the near tragedy, and I remember watching it all unfold on TV until late at night. All the stations were broadcasting the story. Thinking back, I believe that this was the first time in my life that I prayed hard. I was watching the images on the screen and listening to the exchanges

between the ground crew and the three astronauts. I leaned forward, my hands sweating and my eyes fixed. I imagined how the families of these men must have felt, and my entire being began to pray for their safe return. I looked down and saw that without even realizing it, I had clasped my hands in the shape of prayer.

On TV, I saw people from all around the globe, united in praying for these strangers: the pope and all the people gathered around the Vatican, the Jews at the Wailing Wall in Jerusalem, and, if memory serves me correctly, Buddhists in yellow robes somewhere in Asia, and Muslims in the Middle East. It seemed that the entire world was praying for the safety of these astronauts—neither religion nor nationality limited our desire for their safe homecoming.

This could be the first time that so many people across the planet prayed for the same thing at once. The heart of the global community was indeed one at that time. There was no difference between Americans, Soviets, Europeans, Jews, Arabs, or Asians. Everyone was brother and sister. I firmly believe that this is how the astronauts' safe return was made possible.

How can we know how the power of prayer works? I can't explain the mechanism. The one thing I can say with confidence is that when it works in the water, it can actually alter its structure. This means that we've proven that physical energy can change in accordance with our wishes. I've become absolutely convinced of this after carrying out so many experiments where we've prayed over water and actually transformed its crystals into more beautiful forms. This chapter introduces the structure of water before and after prayer to examine how it evolves.

88

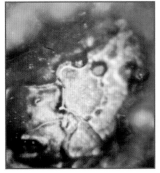

Dam water before the incantations and prayers.

Dam water after the incantations and prayers. A heptagonal crystal appeared as well.

Dam water after the incantations and prayers.

# Incantations and Prayers to the Water of Fujiwara Dam

This is how the water crystal changed after an hour of incantations by Hoki Kato, an ascetic priest of Shingon Tantric Buddhism. The *Kaji* prayer is a service directly transmitted from the ancient priest Kobo Daishi, and involves the light of the Buddha reflecting on the water of the soul, making the supplicant and the Buddha as one. The wish is recited along with the sutra as fire burns.

This experiment was conducted at Fujiwara Dam in Gunma Prefecture in October 1997. I observed it myself,

and it was my first experience in clearly witnessing the power of prayer. You can see the deity's work in the transformation of the crystal's appearance and beauty before and after the incantations. It took me five years to solve the mystery of why this happened.

There are more details about the experiments we conducted here in the Introduction. But for now, I hope you enjoy the heavenly beauty of the final image of the water after the incantations and prayers.

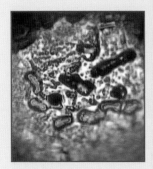

*Left:* The tap water of Asakusabashi, Tokyo, before the prayer.
*Right:* The tap water of Asakusabashi, Tokyo, after the prayer.

90

# The Experiment of Prayer from the Video *The Message from Water*

Having decided that we'd like to show the actual growing of beautiful crystals to the readers of *The Message from Water,* we succeeded in capturing this on film in October 2002. Among the most adventurous was a project of prayer experimentation where everything had to be done in real time in order to be convincing. We had four pairs of parents and children, and each group gave a short prayer (three minutes) to the tap water of Tokyo, which usually never forms crystals. Then, after freezing it for three hours, we videotaped the crystals while the participants were watching via TV monitor. The energy of pure prayer from the children and parents was conveyed beautifully, as you can see in the photo of the tap water after the prayers.

The water from a lake in Carapicuiba before the prayer.

## The Ceremony of Prayer at a Lake in Carapicuiba, Brazil

I was visiting Sao Paulo, Brazil, in November 2002, when I had the opportunity to travel to the bank of a lake in Carapicuiba. The water was terribly polluted, so we performed a purification ceremony through prayer. As you see in the photo, we were just a small group. Therefore, instead of praying to the lake directly, we held hands and prayed as we stood around a bottle of the water.

As a result, the average water crystals before the prayer transformed into the beautiful ones you see on page 92. Not only did the water in the bottle change, but so did the water in the lake, its crystals becoming more lovely after the prayer. The similarity theory of "the part is also the whole; the whole is also the part" was verified.

Water from the lake in Carapicuiba, placed in a bottle and prayed over in the center of the prayer circle (after the prayer).

The water of the lake in Carapicuiba—not in the bottle—after the prayer.

93

# Project Love and Thanks to the Water of the World

At dawn on July 25, 2003, I stood with 200 others by Lake Galilee in Israel, the lake that's famous for its connection with Jesus Christ, and offered a prayer of devout love and thanks to the water. This was part of my Project of Love and Thanks to Water.

On that very day, about 100 teams in 33 countries offered the prayer of love and thanks by their waters in the same way. The participants in the prayers were both people I'd contacted directly during my travels and those supporters who had heard about the project through my Website.

I launched this project with the desire to make real the earnest hopes for peace that I felt when I traveled throughout the world, beginning in March 2000, to give my lectures. On the following pages, I'd like to tell you about some of the results.

94

# The Prayer from Galilee to Tokyo

On the evening before the Project of Love and Thanks to the Water, we asked the 200 participants in my seminar to send prayers from the venue in Israel to a sample of tap water prepared beforehand that was sitting in my office in Tokyo. As you can see, the tap water in Tokyo, which normally never crystalizes, made a beautiful crystal.

The water of Lake Deininger Weiher, before the prayer. Perhaps due to low levels of contaminants in the lake, we've managed to create a lovely crystal.

The water of Lake Deininger Weiher, after the prayer. The magnification was the same as we'd used to photograph the crystal before the prayer, but a larger crystal appeared. I think this means that a lot of energy has been received.

95

# Lake Deininger Weiher, Germany

As the pictures show, this is a beautiful lake in the forest near Munich, Germany, a place with birdsong and children's shouts of joy—perfect for recreation and relaxation for families and lovers. About 250 supporters, many of whom had answered the call to action on my Website, gathered at 7:30 in the evening and offered this prayer of love and thanks to the water:

Wasser, wir lieben Dich (Water, we love you)
Wasser, wir danker Dir (Water, we thank you)
Wasser, wir respektieren Dich (Water, we respect you)

The water of Buan Dam, before the prayer. We were lucky to get just one ring-shaped crystal.

The water of Buan Dam, after the prayer. It turned into a powerful hexagonal crystal.

96

# Buan Dam, Jeollabuk-do, Korea

On the day of Project Love and Thanks to Water (July 25, 2003), a very meaningful event was held at Buan Dam in Korea. There were presentations of songs by children and the floating of paper boats printed with crystal pictures. I hope this kind of ceremony will be held every year. Water is a philosophy that teaches us love and thanks and helps us achieve it—it's our life as well as our friend.

The water of Lake Biwa, before the prayer. Unfortunately, Lake Biwa is still contaminated.

The water of Lake Biwa, after the prayer. We achieved a hexagonal crystal that was incomparably more beautiful than the original form.

The water of Lake Biwa a month after the prayer. Here you can see a heptagonal crystal that is thought to be showing a higher dimension.

97

# Lake Biwa

The result of the Lake Biwa event in 1999, which I discussed in the Introduction of this book, gave us great confidence and encouragement when we revisited the site in 2003 for Project Love and Thanks to Water. It was cloudy that day, but we sent out the energy of prayer and thanks to the lake, which is sometimes called the "Womb of Japan."

Although it wasn't possible to surround the lake in order to conduct the ceremony, we were able to make a hexagon, positioning ourselves at six points: Chikubi island in the north, and on the banks at Imazu, Omi-maiko, Otsu, and Omi-hachiman. We took samples of the water on July 23, a few days before the ceremony; on the evening of July 25, after the prayers; and again one month later, on August 25.

The tap water of Hiroshima Peace Memorial Park, before the prayer. It might be circulated sewer water, because we couldn't find any beautiful crystals.

98

The tap water of Hiroshima Peace Memorial Park, after the prayer. A clear shape of prayer appeared. I think that if we'd had a few more people praying with us, the shape would have grown more perfect.

## Hiroshima Peace Memorial Park

In the morning of July 25, 2003, ten people gathered at the riverbed of the Motoyasu river in front of the skeletal remains that is the monument to the atomic bombing in the center of Hiroshima City. The people held hands with one another and offered a prayer of thanks and peace to the water, which was taken from the pond of the "Flame of Peace" in the park. Nothing changed during the prayer, but the moment the prayer ended, a very heavy rain began to fall. I was overwhelmed with gratitude.

## Diluted and Mixed

We mixed about 30 different kinds of water sent from various places in Japan and around the world, to which had been offered the prayer of love and thanks on July 25, 2003. Since some of the water had a large volume of minerals, we diluted it with distilled water by a thousand to get crystals. This looks similar to the crystal of "Gassho (Hands Joined in Prayer)" from the first chapter of this book. It seems that the result of everyone's positive intentions appeared as the shape of prayer.

*Left:* The water of Won-jok Temple, before the prayer.
*Right:* The water of Won-jok Temple, after the prayer.

## Won-jok Temple, Korea

At Won-jok Temple, a convent in Korea, spring water from the mountains is drawn by the nuns who pray there daily. This is a place where prayers of thanks are offered all the time.

While we obtained no crystals from the mountain spring water, from the water of this "thanksgiving place," the temple, a beautiful crystal was formed. It reminds me of the condensation of the energy of prayer.

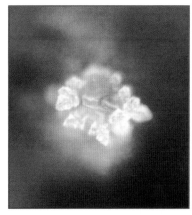

The tap water from an elementary school, before the prayer.

The water from the drainage basin, before the prayer.

The tap water from an elementary school, after the prayer.

The water from the drainage basin, after the prayer.

# Experiment at an Elementary School

In an elementary school where *The Message from Water* had become a topic of conversation, I gave a seminar to some students and showed them my slides of crystal pictures. The children really seemed to understand that language and feelings can be conveyed to water.

At the end of my talk, I asked the children if they'd be careful not to use negative language anymore.

Almost all the students agreed to this. Later, with the support of the kids and teachers, we conducted an experiment of praying to samples of water in the classroom. We used tap water and some water from a drainage basin. It was a great success—the children's pure feelings were clearly conveyed to the water.

After showing the word *love* to the tap water.

After showing the words *love* and *thanks* to the tap water.

102

Tap water, before the experiment.

## <u>Changing Tap Water</u>

I was asked to give a seminar in a town in Japan. I asked the people to send me a sample of their tap water beforehand, so I could take a picture of the crystal formations in the water. As you can see, the results were pretty pathetic. So we decided to take a few more pictures of the same water, this time after attaching the Japanese character for "love" to one and "love and thanks" to the other. The water revived beautifully.

Crystals typically found in ordinary distilled water.

103

## SARS

Awhile back, when there were several outbreaks of severe acute respiratory syndrome, or SARS, we showed a sample of water the acronym in both English and Japanese and photographed the resulting crystals. Oddly, the crystals we found didn't appear any different than those we normally find in distilled water.

After we showed the words *jusho-kyusei-kokyuki-shokogun* (severe acute respiratory syndrome) to the water for 24 hours, we found these deformed crystals.

I thought about it for a while, and then I asked my staff to try the same experiment once more—but this time, using the full name of the syndrome, not the abbreviation. As you can see in the photos, we didn't find any well-formed crystals in these samples.

When we showed "Severe Acute Respiratory Syndrome" in English, we noticed that the water formed similar misshapen crystals.

The distorted crystals transformed themselves into beautiful formations after we replaced the label with *ai kansha,* which means "love and thanks" in Japanese.

Next, we peeled the "Severe Acute Respiratory Syndrome" labels off the water bottles and replaced them with labels in that read "Love and Thanks" in both English and Japanese. As the pictures show, these words in both languages yielded beautiful crystal formations.

105

These are crystals that were shown "Love & Thanks" in English. They're strikingly similar to those formed by the same words in Japanese.

This experiment really reinforces my new ideas about water, which are as follows:

- Water catches the vibrations of words and reflects them back in the form of crystals.

- As long as a word is used correctly, the reaction of water will be the same, regardless of language.

- It's better to be as precise as possible, as water is very sensitive to vibrations. (For example, using "Severe Acute Respiratory Syndrome" instead of "SARS" allowed the water to absorb the meaning of the words.)

- The words *love* and *thanks* have very positive energy.

- Even if damaged, water can regain positive energy.

Man is mostly made of water. Therefore, it seems logical that we have the physical characteristics described in the preceding list as well. If we accept this, then we have to believe that there's still hope for our world.

107

## Love and Thanks

Obtaining the crystal of "Love and Thanks" changed my vision of the cosmos. I realized that these words formed the most beautiful crystal of any taken to this date. The concept of love and thanks is the idea behind the universe, God's benevolent intention. I was shown in a real, pure, and profound vision that the active energy of love and the passive energy of thanks resonate together, and that this is how the universe was created.

Prayer conducted while holding hands.

108

## Energy Differs Depending on the Shape of Prayer

The shape of prayer that was introduced in Chapter 1 was that of praying hands. This seems to be a universal shape of prayer for humankind. The style varies slightly—some people lace their fingers so that their hands are as one, some press their palms together, and others hold their hands above their heads before bringing them down to the ground—but essentially the shape is the same.

We carried out an experiment to see if there was any difference in the crystals when we held hands with others in prayer as opposed to praying while clasping our own hands together, without touching anyone else. The experiment was conducted under stable conditions in the same location, with the same subjects, distilled water, and photographer.

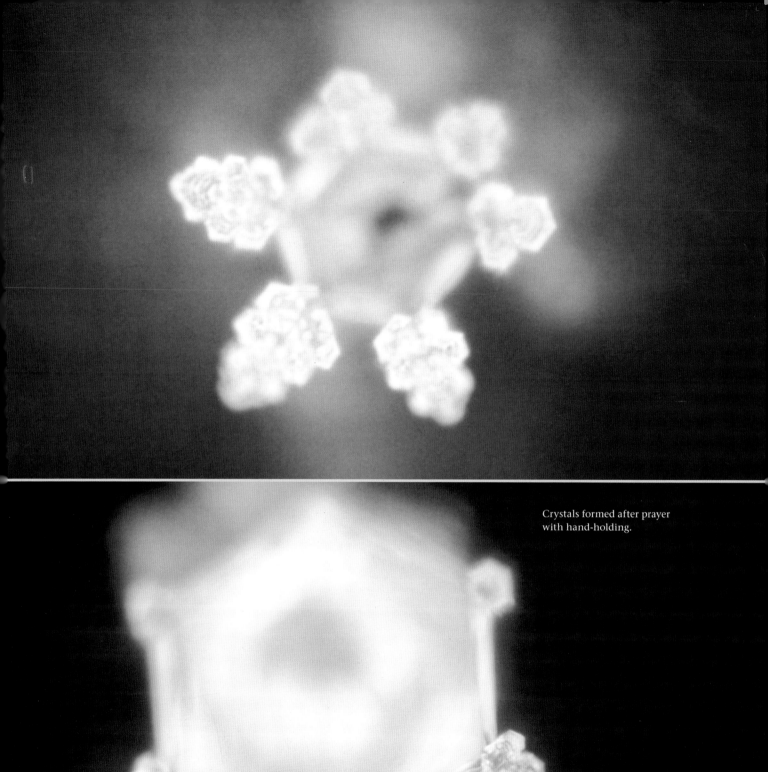

Crystals formed after prayer
with hand-holding.

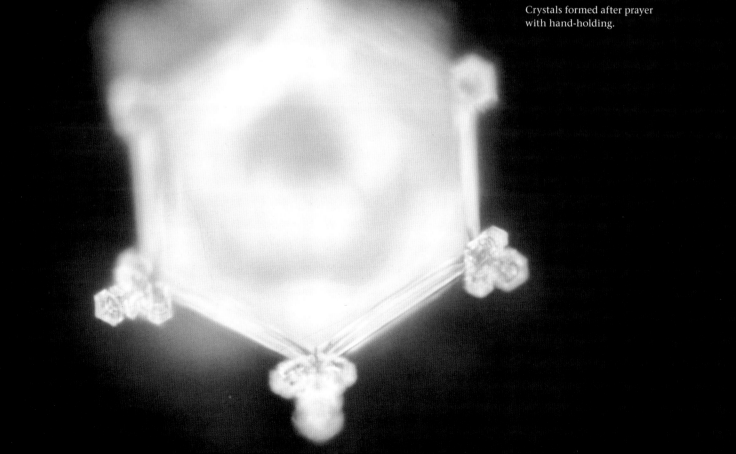

Prayer conducted while pressing palms together.

110

Crystals formed after praying with the palms together.

As you can see, we could clearly obtain more beautiful crystals when prayer was conducted with the palms of each individual pressed together in the prayer position. This posture is obviously full of positive energy.

When I asked the participants how they felt during the experiment, they all said that with palms together, they were able to concentrate better and didn't feel as many distractions. Since this experiment, I've been praying with my palms together every day, and I encourage those around me to do the same.

✳✳✳  ✳✳✳

111

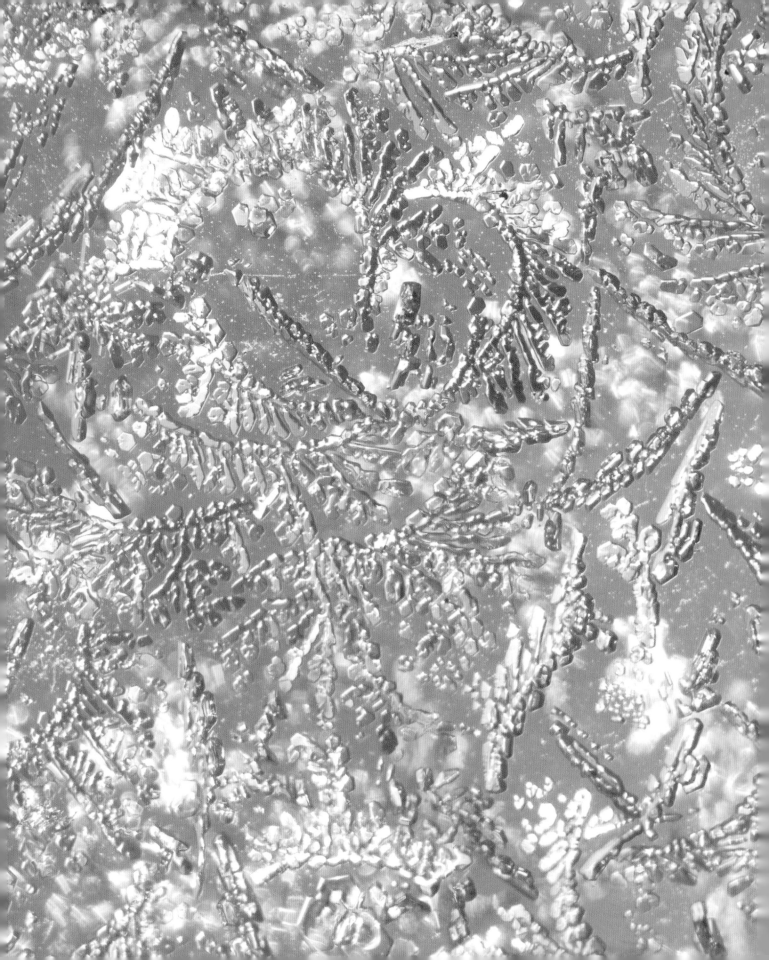

# AFTERWORD

My grandson, who is growing up well. He's now bigger than the kitty.

I think that humanity is currently at an important crossroads. The wave of terrorism, in particular the tragic attacks of September 11, 2001, is far from losing energy; rather it's expanding in both area and number of victims. Even Japan, which has been proud of its domestic peace and order, has felt compelled to get involved in this struggle.

The United States is fighting hard under the flag of freedom for world peace. Unfortunately, the approach they took may have completely awoken the anti-American forces throughout the world and given rise to rebellion. At this point, it looks as if the fight may last until one side gets knocked down for the count.

We can't allow this to happen, whatever the cost. If such a war continues and escalates to such a catastrophic extent, the earth won't be able to sustain its strength. The negative waves of menace will completely destroy the crystals of all water, the breath and blood of all life on this planet.

Moreover, if this happens, it will become a global epidemic. The result will be unlike any plague or disaster the world has ever seen. This is because the world's population was less than 180 million before the first century. In 1900, there were about 1.5 billion people; in 1950, 2.5 billion; and at present, there are 6.3 billion people on this planet.

This means that there's been a 3.8 billion increase in the last 50 years. This is absurdly abnormal. The population increased far too quickly, depleting and abusing energy. The result of this depletion is heat, which has led to the temperature of the Earth rising. Earth has actually become ill, the way a person would. This means that the immune system of the Earth, the mother of humanity, has been depleted down to a level that's barely sustainable.

Who caused this situation? It's no single person's fault. Rather, it's our collective responsibility. But this is no reason to feel defeated, or to wake up in the morning with a feeling of helplessness. As I've

shown through this photo collection, the pure prayer for peace can bring the miracle of Apollo 13 to all humanity.

Let us pray together. Let us put our hands together. Just 30 seconds a day is all it takes. This is the message from water.

✳✳✳ ✳✳✳

114

# APPENDIX

## Crystal Photography in the Laboratory

*Contributed by Takashige Kizu, Manager, IHM Research Institute*

The crystal pictures you see in this photo album are prepared using the following procedure. In this section, I'll explain crystal observation in general and note the different trends of crystal patterns obtained from each sample, using as an example the observations from the Sukato Temple, which is featured in Chapter 2 of this book.

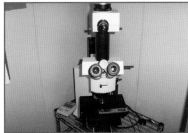
Picture 1

### The Procedure for Freezing the Specimen (Water)

1. From each sample, 0.5cc of water is dropped onto 50 separate plastic petri dishes using a syringe (picture 1).

2. The petri dishes are then covered and stored in a freezer that's capable of cooling to at least -25°C (-13°F).

3. The samples are frozen for three hours.

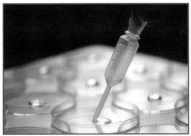
Picture 2

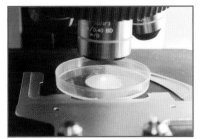
Picture 3

### The Procedure for Taking Crystal Pictures

1. Frozen crystal samples are observed in a large refrigerated room set at a temperature of -5°C (23°F).

2. The microscope used for observation is a metal light microscope with a camera (picture 2).

3. The frozen sample has a swelling in the middle (picture 3), and it's on that swelling that light is projected down from the microscope (picture 4).

Picture 4

115

4. The crystals are observed through the eyepiece and photographed by the camera mounted on the microscope. The equipment used for the crystal photography is an Olympus System Metal Light Microscope BX60 and an Olympus Full Automatic Photomicroscope PM10SP. We use Fujicolor professional-quality Negative Color Film ISO400.

### Observation Criteria

First, all 50 samples of crystals are classified according to their shape (beautiful, semi-beautiful, hexagonal, radial, lattice, irregular, collapsed, none).

Next, each type of crystal shape is assigned a score from 0 to 100. The score of each sample observed is added up and the average score of the 50 specimens from the total points becomes the crystal evaluation score.

The scoring criteria is based on whether the crystal is hexagonal or not, as well as whether it's beautiful or not, based on the judgment of an observer. (For example, a beautiful hexagonal crystal gets the maximum score of 100 points, while if there are no crystal formations, the score is 0).

Although this method of calculating the evaluation score is subjective, I believe it still reveals the overall trend of the crystallization of the water sample.

116

## Water Crystals of the Sukato Temple

Now let's see the method in action. The table and graph seen here present the observations gathered from the rainwater left in three jars in and around the Sukato Temple. The greater the number of beautiful crystals observed, the higher the evaluation score will be. Furthermore, the amount of crystals in the beautiful and semi-beautiful categories shows us that the rainwater left in the temple and in the forest have a much greater chance of yielding beautiful crystals than the rainwater left in the village. It's from this data that we draw conclusions about the varying energy levels of each location.

117

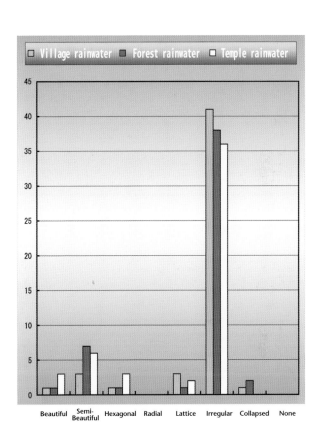

Water Crystals of the Sukato Temple

| Samples | Beautiful | Semi-beautiful | Hexagonal | Radial | Lattice | Irregular | Collapsed | None | Multiple |
|---|---|---|---|---|---|---|---|---|---|
| A  Village rainwater | 1 | 3 | 1 | 0 | 3 | 41 | 1 | 0 | 28.8 |
| B  Forest rainwater | 1 | 7 | 1 | 0 | 1 | 38 | 2 | 0 | 38.2 |
| C  Temple rainwater | 3 | 6 | 3 | 0 | 2 | 36 | 0 | 0 | 41.8 |

# ABOUT THE AUTHOR

**Masaru Emoto** was born in Yokohama, Japan, in July 1943. He's a graduate of the Yokohama Municipal University's Department of Humanities and Sciences with a focus on international relations. In 1986 he established the IHM Corporation in Tokyo. In October of 1992, he received certification from the Open International University as a doctor of alternative medicine. Subsequently, he was introduced to the concept of micro-cluster water in the U.S., and Magnetic Resonance Analysis technology. The quest thus began to discover the mystery of water.

He undertook extensive research of water around the planet, not so much as a scientific researcher, but more from the perspective of an original thinker. At length he realized that it was in the frozen crystal form that water showed us its true nature. He continues with this experimentation and has written a variety of well-received books in Japanese, as well as the seminal *Message from Water,* now published in 23 languages. He also wrote *The Hidden Messages in Water* and *The True Power of Water.*

✳✳✳  ✳✳✳

**Many thanks for the use of these references:**

CD: *The Glorious History of Black Music*/Amuse Media • *Lennon Legend*/Toshiba-EMI Ltd. • *Tendai Shomyo, Kongokai Mandala Kyo*/ Denon Ltd. • *At the Shore—Best Collection,* by Suzan Osbourne/Canyon International • *All about Kimigayo*/King Records • *Christmas Best/String Orchestra*/CX130 Stereo

Book: *World Heritage*/Shobunsha Publications, Inc. • *Complete Japanese Art Works, Mandala and Raigozu*/ Kodansha Publishers Ltd. • *World Heritage Map,* Colin Wilson/Sanseido Publishing Co., Ltd.

Miscellaneous: *Kyureifu,* Osama Inoue • Landscape pictures of Sukato Temple—photographer: Masashi Kawaguchi • The character "Wa"—calligrapher: Shofu Wakayama • "The Power of Words" (pictures of fruit experiment): Madoka Miyako

# HAY HOUSE TITLES OF RELATED INTEREST

## Books

*Crystal Therapy,* by Doreen Virtue, Ph.D., and Judith Lukomski

*Energy Secrets,* by Alla Svirinskaya

*Secrets of the Lost Mode of Prayer,* by Gregg Braden

*Practical Praying* (book-with-CD), by John Edward

*Prayer and the Five Stages of Healing,* by Ron Roth, Ph.D.

*Secrets & Mysteries of the World,* by Sylvia Browne

*Silent Power* (book-with-CD), by Stuart Wilde

## Card Decks

*Healing Cards,* by Caroline Myss and Peter Occhiogrosso

*Inner Peace Cards,* by Dr. Wayne W. Dyer

*Messages from Your Angels Oracle Cards,* by Doreen Virtue, Ph.D.

❂ ❂ ❂

All of the above are available at your local bookstore, or may be ordered by visiting:
Hay House USA: **www.hayhouse.com;** Hay House Australia: **www.hayhouse.com.au;**
Hay House UK: **www.hayhouse.co.uk;** Hay House South Africa: **orders@psdprom.co.za**

❂ ❂ ❂